A Family Treasury of
MYTHS
from
Around
the World

A Family Treasury of MYTHS from Around the World

Retold by

VIVIANE KOENIG

Translated from the French by

ANTHONY ZIELONKA

Illustrated by

VÉRONIQUE AGEORGES

VIVIANE KOENIG

DANIEL HÉNON

HARRY N. ABRAMS, INC., PUBLISHERS

We like to share stories with our children that will enable them to have dreams, give them reassurance and knowledge, and above all, provide them with an irresistible desire to read. But where can we find such masterpieces? It is really not that difficult. There are thousands of them all over the world. Intensely vivid, intelligent, funny, moving, terrifying, and ultimately uplifting, these stories have crossed the centuries and the oceans.

Since the earliest times, human beings have created their own explanations for the movement of the sun, for earthquakes, for heat waves and floods, for their anxieties and their hopes, through stories in which revered gods, admired heroes, cunning animals, and feared monsters confront one another.

From one generation to the next, these marvelous legends have been passed on and today make up an invaluable inheritance, an inheritance that we must continue to share with one another.

Tremble before the wrath of Ra, the Egyptian sun god. Weep with Helios, the Greek god of the sun. Sulk with Amaterasu, the beautiful Japanese goddess. Follow Moses as he journeys toward the Promised Land. Tremble with Ulysses as he listens to the singing of the sirens. Listen to the cries of the infants Romulus and Remus. Meet the wise man who survived the African flood. Learn why hens lay eggs. Venture into the depths of the Indian jungle to meet an arrogant elephant. Beware of the jealous rage of the giant serpent Apophis.

All of these legends have lasted for hundreds, and sometimes thousands of years. They are profound and full of meaning. Reaching back into the roots of old civilizations, the simple and precise words of these stories are deeply moving. In order for us to more fully under- stand the tales, the drawings in this book borrow elements from ancient styles, yet they are enlivened with colors that are clearly modern. So, open your eyes, ears, and heart, and set off on a journey to the land of eternal legends.

Contents

III. The Epics of Heroes

IV. The Sun Gods

Moses
in Egypt

Illustrated by
VIVIANE KOENIG

Night fell a long time ago over Egypt, and yet Pharaoh, the powerful king, is unable to fall asleep.

Since daybreak he has been calling in his best advisers.

"Listen," he tells them, "the Hebrews, my own slaves, are becoming more numerous and more powerful with every passing day. Their growing strength worries me. Tire them out! Load them down with work so I may finally live in peace!"

At once, the King's terrible orders are carried out. Under a blazing sun, the Hebrews are forced to make bricks, build cities, and plow the fields. They work from dawn till dusk and they get very little to eat.

The merciless guards make life harsh for the slaves.

"Fear has still not left my heart," Pharaoh admits to his advisers some time later. I grow more afraid of them every day. I have heard that they are waiting for a liberator. We must prevent them from ever finding such a leader. All of their sons must be drowned the day they are born!

The very next day, the heartless soldiers kill all the young Hebrew boys. However, one slave manages to hide her newborn son for three months. When he grows too large for her to hide him any longer, she places him in a basket of papyrus fiber, kisses him tenderly, and sets him down among the reeds by the banks of the great river.

The current gently carries him away.

Not far from there, Pharaoh's daughter is bathing. Suddenly, she notices the basket and sends her faithful servant to fetch it.

"It is a little Hebrew boy," the

princess murmurs, taking him into her arms.

"How good-looking he is! I shall bring him up myself and call him Moses!"

In the royal palace, the years go by. Moses grows up as a prince of Egypt and becomes a wise, just, and good man. One day, while strolling outside the fortified walls of the city, he enters a construction site where hundreds of Hebrews are working. He sees a guard cruelly beating one of them and decides to defend the slave. Moses strikes the guard with such strength that he kills him. Fearing that Pharaoh will punish him, Moses buries the Egyptian in the sands of the desert and runs away. Day after day, Moses walks through the desert in the direction of the rising sun until he reaches the land of Midian.

Many years later, having become a shepherd, Moses marries the beautiful Zipporah. He has found peace and happiness while the Hebrews continue to suffer as slaves in Egypt. God hears their complaints and sees their tears.

One day, while he is grazing his sheep, Moses sees an angel in the middle of a burning bush. Cautiously, he approaches and sees that the flames are not destroying the bush. He then hears the voice of God calling to him. Terrified, Moses hides his face.

"Moses," orders the Lord, "you must return to Egypt. You will set the Hebrews free and lead them to a land flowing with milk and honey."

"Who am I to do such things?" asks Moses timidly.

"Do not be afraid of anything. I shall be with you," replies the Lord. "Look at the staff that you are holding in your hand and throw it onto the ground." Moses obeys and the staff turns into a snake.

"Seize it!" orders the Lord. Moses complies and the snake becomes a stick again. Without a moment's hesitation, Moses leaves with his wife, his children, and God's staff.

When he arrives at the royal palace, which he knows so well from his childhood, Moses bows before the Pharaoh.

"Your Majesty," he says humbly, "the Lord, who is the God of the Hebrews, asks that you allow his people to leave."

"Who is this Lord I am to obey by freeing my slaves?" shouts the enraged Pharaoh. "I do not know him and I shall not let the Hebrews go."

At that moment, Moses throws his staff down at Pharaoh's feet and the staff turns into a snake.

Frightened by such a miracle, the king summons his magicians. They rush in and they too transform their staffs into snakes! But Moses' snake swallows up all the others and then becomes a staff again. And yet Pharaoh's heart remains hardened to the Hebrews' plight, and he does not release them. So the Lord decides he must force the king to obey him.

"May the waters of the river be turned to blood!" orders the Lord. "The fish will die and the Egyptians will no longer be able to drink the water!"

But Pharaoh's heart is unmoved. And in spite of the wash of blood that flows all over the land, he still does not release his slaves.

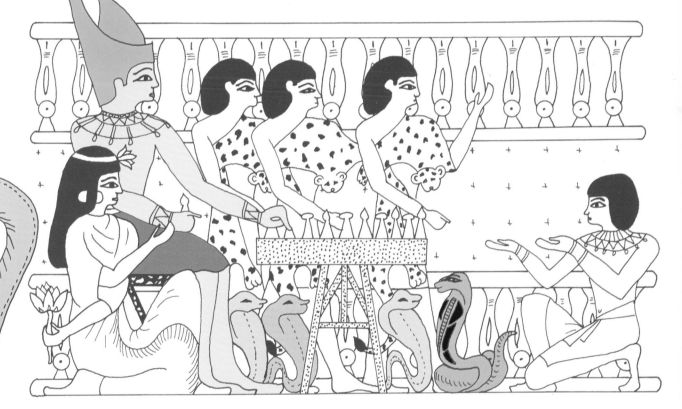

M ay the river be filled with frogs! Let them invade the palace, the houses, and the ovens," orders the Lord.

Tormented by this new affliction, Pharaoh says to Moses, "If your God can get rid of the frogs, I shall allow the Hebrews to leave."

But once the frogs have gone, Pharaoh remains hardened and does not let his slaves go.

"Moses!" orders the Lord,
"Strike the dust of Egypt with your staff.
May it be transformed into vermin!"

"Watch out, Pharaoh, for it
is the hand of God at work here," say
the royal counselors.

But Pharaoh still does not release his slaves.

"May Egypt be invaded by wild animals,"
proclaims the Lord.

Anxiously, Pharaoh says to Moses, "I shall allow the
Hebrews to leave as soon as these animals have gone."

But once the animals have disappeared,
Pharaoh's heart is still as hard as before, and he does
not release his slaves.

"May the horses, donkeys, oxen, and sheep
die," orders the Lord.

With this, Pharaoh still will not
give the Hebrews their freedom.

Moses," orders the Lord, "throw soot up at the sky and blisters shall appear on the people throughout the land." Suddenly finding themselves covered with blisters, the royal counselors are unable to appear before the king, but Pharaoh's heart is still hardened, and he does not release his slaves.

"May a hailstorm rain down on Egypt. Human beings, animals, and plants shall all die," decrees the Lord.

Overwhelmed by this disaster, Pharaoh feels remorse. He says to Moses, "I have behaved badly. My people and I were wrong. If this tempest ends, I shall allow you to leave, taking the Hebrews with you."

The hailstorm ends, but still as unsympathetic as before, Pharaoh does not release his slaves.

"May locusts destroy the crops that were spared by the hail," orders the Lord.

Locusts invade the land and they devour all the fields and the orchards.

"Please, please, may your Lord send away these insects and I shall let you go," Pharaoh implores Moses.

Then God sends down a violent wind that sweeps the locusts away to the sea and drowns them. But God hardens Pharaoh's heart, so the Hebrews may one day tell their children of these trials, and Pharaoh does not release his slaves.

ay night fall over the land," orders the Lord. "May a profound darkness reign over Egypt for three days and three nights, except over the Hebrews, above whom the sun will continue to shine brightly."

"Go and worship your God," says Pharaoh. "Your children may follow you. But your flocks must remain here!"

"We shall not leave without our animals," replies Moses. At this, God once again hardens Pharaoh's heart and he does not release his slaves.

Finally, the Lord says to Moses, "Tell the Pharaoh that I shall kill the eldest son of every family in Egypt.

The sons of princes and
the sons of servants, they shall
all die! To protect themselves, my
people must select a lamb. When evening
comes, they should slit its throat and dab
their doorposts with the blood so I will know
not to enter their homes. Roast the lamb and
eat it quickly with unleavened bread."

"This very night, I shall strike."

At daybreak, Pharaoh is crazed with grief
at his dead son's bedside.

Struck in his very heart, he cries out to Moses,
"Go out into the desert and worship your God.
Take your children, your flocks, but leave
now."

Immediately, the Hebrews set out on
their journey toward the land that God
promised them.

Pharaoh soon regrets the decision he has made, "What have I done," he exclaims. "I have just released these slaves who served me so well. Prepare six hundred chariots with my best officers at once. We must capture them!"

A few hours later, while encamped by the shores of the Red Sea, the Hebrews watch with terror as the Egyptian army draws near.

"Why did you lead us out of Egypt?" they ask Moses. "We would have been better off serving Pharaoh than dying here."

"Do not be afraid," replies Moses, "for God is fighting on your side."

A great silence greets his words. Then the Lord says to Moses,

"Raise your staff and the sea will open up."

Moses does as God has told him to do. A violent wind blows up, parting the waters, and the waves form two gigantic walls. The Lord guides the Hebrews between the walls, and they continue forward on land that is now dry.

The Egyptians immediately set off after them. But the Lord watches over his people and he commands the waters to flow together again. As the massive watery walls close, the sea swallows up Pharaoh's entire army. Meanwhile, on the opposite shore, the Hebrews continue on their journey toward the land flowing with milk and honey.

They sing songs praising
the glory of the Lord,
overjoyed to finally have
their freedom.

Illustrated by
VÉRONIQUE AGEORGES

Izanagi and Izanami

In the blue, balmy, infinite heavens, the eight million Japanese gods have lived for a long, long time. How handsome, great, and powerful they are. Smiling serenely, with their dark, mysterious eyes and their clothes of vibrantly colored silks, they are simply radiant!

The gods decide to create a new world and ask two of the youngest gods to carry out the task.

"Handsome Izanagi and you, charming Izanami, make for us a marvelous world like the one that already exists in our dreams." The god Izanagi is a handsome, bearded man with long fine hair. Izanami is a ravishing goddess with exquisite eyes. Happy and proud to have been chosen, they accept this difficult task. Before leaving heaven, they pause for a few moments on a floating bridge suspended from the sky. Its fine colors form a magnificent rainbow that is luminous and enchanting.

"How should we create the world?" they wonder. The red band on which their feet are resting turns orange, then blue, then indigo, then violet. They are dreaming.

Above them, the sky is immense. Below them, lies the limitless ocean. Izanagi thrusts his golden lance downward and gently stirs up the freezing waters. Then he moves the waters faster and faster, forming a fine, white foam that bubbles up, thickens, and becomes land. A minute island rises up and beautiful sea birds come to rest upon it.

**The two deities step down from
their rainbow and set foot on the first
island of the new world.**

They are happy there. They gossip, express their love for
each other, and spend some delightful moments together.
Their happiness increases with the birth of each of their
many children. They are wonderful children—Amaterasu,
the sun goddess; Susanoo, the god of storms; and the
divinities of the moon, of the trees and rocks, of the flowers
and of fire, of the mountains and rivers, of the cherry
trees and animals, of men and women, and of all the
Japanese islands.

How beautiful, strong, and graceful they all are," the bearded Izanagi says, as he watches his children with delight. "Of course, they often quarrel, but that should not worry you, my gentle Izanami. Everything will be fine."

"Alas! I get more and more worried every day," sighs Izanami, as she rearranges a long wisp of her silky hair. "Susanoo's antics upset me terribly. He is destroying the dikes in the rice fields, which were so painstakingly planted. He fills up the ditches that people have dug. He walks around the land shouting and waving his sharp sword at everyone he meets. He is exasperating both the gods and the humans. I wonder whether he will ever calm down."

"He is abusing his power as god of the storms and master of the Sea of Eight Hundred Thousand Waves."

Time goes by but, unfortunately, nothing changes. Susanoo devises more and more silly pranks. One day, he pays a surprise visit to his sister, the sun goddess Amaterasu. Sitting comfortably in her pure and sacred room, Amaterasu is dreaming. She is surrounded by her faithful companions, who are spinning linen and weaving clothes for the gods. Suddenly, her brother bursts into the room, noisy, violent, and screaming wildly.

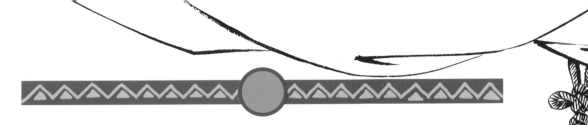

Knocking over everything that stands in his way, he flails his arms and lets out a horrible cackle.

All the panic-stricken women run away except Amaterasu.

Hurt and furious at her brother for behaving so badly, the majestic goddess turns her back on him and decides to lock herself away in her heavenly cave.

"I shall remain hidden for as long as the eight million gods put up with my brother's incredible behavior," Amaterasu cries out from heaven. Her eyes gleam with a thousand sparks, and her hair moves with the halting rhythm of her words. She clenches her fists.

Overcome with anger,
Amaterasu goes into her cave,
rolls a heavy rock to block the entrance,
and thereby plunges the world
into darkness.

The sun has disappeared! Shadows
cover the Earth. People and animals are
worried. Plants do not grow. Flowers no longer
open. The birds no longer sing. Days resemble
nights. All is sadness and desolation. Feeling their way
around, the eight million gods move across the vast plain
of heaven and they all come together to decide what
should be done.

"How can we calm the sun goddess?" asks one god.
"How can we get her to come back out?" responds
another.

Izanami and Izanagi do not know
what to say. They are very ashamed
of Susanoo.

By the light of the full moon, all the gods gather to look into the flames of a burning stag to foresee the future. They call out to the god of cunning, who at once thinks up a plan.

"Blacksmith god, make us a magnificent mirror!" he orders. "And you, goddesses endowed with the most skillful of fingers, thread together these gems and create the most beautiful piece of jewelry and attach it to the branches of the Sacred Tree. You, goddess with the gentle voice, recite some poems. You, goddess with the light feet, adorn your hair with flowers and place a beautiful vase in front of Amaterasu's cave, together with a tuft of heavenly bamboo shoots. Then you must start dancing."

The gods are enthusiastic. The goddess with the light feet begins to dance faster and faster, and the whole heavenly plain becomes animated. Happiness returns at last, and the eight million gods burst out in joyful laughter. Alone in her cave, radiant with light, Amaterasu wonders what it is that the gods are finding so amusing outside in the darkness. Curious, she takes a few small steps toward the entrance of her cave and pushes aside the heavy rock just enough to see out. Through the crack she sees the offerings of the gods—a mirror, jewelry, the heavenly bamboo, the vase.

"How beautiful they are!" she exclaims, laughing. But her laughter stops short, before it has hardly left her mouth. The mirror is reflecting the most beautiful of goddesses, and she is overcome with jealousy.

"**W**ho dares to rival my beauty. I have always been without equal," she thinks anxiously.

Now desperate to see more, Amaterasu rolls the stone a little farther. Taking a few small, furtive steps, she comes out and once again floods the world with her light. At last the day is dawning! But Amaterasu does not care about that. She has forgotten Susanoo, her anger, and her solitary cave.

"Who is this beautiful woman?" she murmurs as she approaches the mysterious mirror.

The mirror is there, almost within her reach. She rushes forward and grabs it suddenly, and then realizes it is her own reflection that she found so enchanting. Relieved, this most beautiful woman accepts the offerings and smiles at the eight million gods.

"Oh, Amaterasu, come back with us!" they implore her humbly. "Your brother, Susanoo, will get the punishment he deserves. He will never bother you again on the plains of heaven. We have banished him to Earth forever."

From that day forward, the sun goddess has been shining in the skies, far away from her mischievous brother, who amuses himself by stirring up storms, tidal waves, and floods. Amaterasu has won. When asked if she is the most powerful of the eight million Japanese gods, she replies, "The most powerful and the most beautiful!" without a moment's hesitation.

Illustrated by
DANIEL HÉNON

The Sparrow and the Hen

Two sparrows with soft and silky feathers live just outside a small village in the heart of Africa. They lead a tranquil life in their old nest because it is well hidden in the branches of the thick baobab tree.

They like to hear the rustling of the leaves when the breeze blows, the splashing drops of water when the rain falls, and the gossiping of the villagers who pass by. Our sparrows often venture out into the village, where they always find a few leftovers to peck away at. But they are always careful to fly away swiftly whenever the children are playing, running, or shouting near them.

Near the pond, the Crested Crane, with her long, thin legs, warned them of the dangers of these young humans. She said they would hold you down by your legs and tear your feathers out with frightening speed.

"Watch out, watch out!" she repeats.

Gray Parrot adds that the adult humans are even more dangerous. They catch you by the tail, twist your neck, and pluck out all your feathers before dropping you into a pot of boiling water.

"Watch out, watch out!" he repeats.

T hese terrible stories make the feathers on the heads of our poor sparrows stand on end. Frightened, they fly away as soon as a human approaches them. Sometimes they even shiver just at the thought of being caught.

"Be careful . . ."

But one day, while they are hopping around looking for twigs, bits of dry grass, and feathers to strengthen their old nest, they meet the adorable red-feathered Little Hen. Plump, smiling, and sweet, she waddles along without a care on the edge of the field and far away from the village, pecking at a few crunchy grains. Suddenly, two women in brightly colored clothes come up to her.

"Come, Little Hen, fly away with us," chirps

one of the sparrows. "Don't stay on the ground, it's dangerous."

"How horrible, I hate flying," she replies, nodding her head gently. Then she admits with a sigh, "I don't even know how to fly! I have never bothered to learn how."

"Well, you have short legs and long wings like we do," cry the sparrows, who are already flying more than five feet above the ground.

"Try flapping your wings gently, then faster and faster, and as soon as a breeze blows over you . . . up you'll fly! See how much fun it is!"

ittle Hen raises her head, blinks, sees the two women who are coming dangerously close to her, and cackles, "I hate your stupid games and I refuse to fly with you. The wind might tangle up my fine red feathers, which I smooth out so carefully every morning. My fiancé, the rooster waiting for me over there, will protect me. Goodbye!"

"Little Hen, quick! They are coming. Fly away! The three of us will have fun together. We will play at follow the leader and Simon says. We will fly around the trees and pick out tasty earthworms from under the leaves."

But Little Hen is not listening
to them. She is moving as fast as her
little clawed feet will carry her away from
the village women and toward her rooster friend.
"Stupid bird," shouts one of the disappointed
sparrows, "watch out for the humans."

**"One day you will not be able to run away
and you will be eaten!"**

"Poor little anxious sparrows! If you are so
scared, just stay perched in your tree!" replies
Little Hen with disdain, "and let me peck
away and live as I choose to."

The days and weeks go by. Little Hen is doing very well and is becoming more and more plump under her beautiful, silky feathers. Her cheeks are getting rounder. Her eyes are shining. The rooster adores her plump and bright red body. She has long since forgotten the prudent words of the sparrows when, one evening, a man from the village comes slowly up to her, holding a stick behind his back.

"Pretty bird, pretty bird, come here!" he says. "You are so beautiful. My eyes are so pleased to see you, and soon my stomach will be pleased to taste you!"

"How good you will be in some rich stock!"

At once, Little Hen understands the danger and runs as fast as possible to seek shelter in the tall grasses. But her large stomach slows her down. She feels her heart beating faster and faster.

S he sees the rooster, who is perched on a rooftop made of banana tree leaves, and she cries out to him, "What is going to happen to me? I should have listened to the sparrows' wise advice. I am going to die in a pot full of vegetables. I am too big to fly now. I flap my wings but nothing happens."

"Remain calm, my favorite Little Hen. I will find a way to save you," declares the rooster. "Look at me! I wake the villagers up at dawn with my piercing crowing. Why don't you follow my example? You too must have a special gift. You could . . ."

But he cannot think of anything. He ruffles up his multicolored feathers and looks sadly into the distance.

Meanwhile, the man with the stick has found Little Hen and catches her by her feet. Terror-stricken, Little Hen wriggles and manages to escape, and again she hides in the long grass. Finally, the sun disappears under the horizon.

The darkness of night protects the careless little hen.

Exhausted and trembling with fear, she collapses beneath a baobab tree. She looks up and sees the two sparrows, who are now singing in full voice.

"Little Hen," one of the sparrows chirps out to her, "Lay an egg that is so appetizing and large that it will make the man with the stick feel hungry."

Huddled up in the tall grass, Little Hen at last has the solution to her problem. Her heart jumps with joy. The warm and gentle night envelops her. For the moment she is safe.

"Tomorrow, she will be just as good, and maybe even better," sighs the man with the stick as he returns to his hut.

Early the next morning, the man with the stick finds Little Hen sleeping peacefully at the foot of an old tree stump.

He walks up to her
without making any noise.

"I have wasted enough time with you,
my sweet little bird!" he says.
"I am hungry. Don't make me
wait any longer!"

T hen, very calmly, Little Hen gets up and reveals a beautiful, warm egg, with a smooth, speckled, orange-colored shell.

"What a marvelous egg you have laid!" shouts the man. "It is absolutely perfect. I will boil it, put some salt on it, and eat it at once."

The man eats the egg and his hunger is satisfied.

From now on, Little Hen sleeps snuggled up against a tree stump, her mind at rest. Every morning, when the rooster calls out with his piercing cry, she leaves a beautiful, fresh egg for the villagers. To thank her for this gift, they throw down a few grains of corn for her to eat and forbid the children to bother her.

"Little Hen, don't go away," they say, smiling at her. "Please stay in our village."

Ever since that day, hens have been laying eggs that delight humans. It hardly matters that they still cannot fly, and that they like to eat as much as they do!

Illustrated by
VÉRONIQUE AGEORGES

How the Elephant Was Punished

In the land of the elephants, at the very heart of the Indian jungle, a gigantic tree stands, protecting a very small nest from the wind and the sun. It was in this tiny nest, held up by the delicate foliage, that Little Bird, with her silky plumage, placed her eggs. She watches over them night and day with infinite care and love.

One day, Large Elephant,
with his long trunk and his small ears,
approaches Little Bird's tree.

The heat bothers the enormous beast, the insects
annoy him, and his skin itches. Very irritated, he
scratches his back against Little Bird's tree. The eggs
begin to roll around dangerously in their cozy nest.

"Mr. Large Elephant, have pity on us, please!"
pleads Little Bird in a terrified voice. "Stop shaking
my tree. My eggs might fall!"

ut Large Elephant does not listen. He continues to scratch his back against the bark so vigorously that, one by one, the eggs fall to the ground and break. Stricken with grief, Little Bird sobs as she hops around among the smashed eggshells. She bumps into thin blades of dried grass and curses the large animal who is responsible for her misfortune. Large Elephant cannot hear or even see her. He is already lumbering away, with his heavy stride, back to his herd.

"I shall fight and defeat you, thoughtless Large Elephant!"

"You will be my enemy forever," swears Little Bird as she watches him gently sway his ridiculous tail, with its thick, dark hairs.

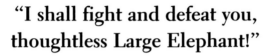

In despair, Little Bird flies to see her friend Yellow Parrot. "Large Elephant smashed all my eggs," she laments. "I am so unhappy."

"Could you invent some scheme to get back at him?"

"Alas," replies Yellow Parrot, "it is very dangerous for weak animals like us to wage war against such a bad-mannered elephant. However, nothing can beat intelligence and cunning. My friend Striped Bee is marvelously wise. Let's go and see if she can help us."

The two birds fly off at once over the jungle, avoiding Bengal Tiger, swooping above the rice field, and landing on the highest branch of Striped Bee's honey tree. Little Bird tells her the whole unhappy adventure. Striped Bee reflects for a long time, buzzes, flies around collecting nectar from nearby flowers, and then comes back to the two birds.

"Near the rice field, in the middle of the lotus flowers, lives the cunning Green Frog," she says. "She knows how to solve all kinds of problems. Let's go and see her."

Little Bird, Yellow Parrot, and Striped Bee fly to the rice field and tell Green Frog about the problem.
"Little Bird, be brave!" she says softly. "Cunning is much more effective than anger. In order to punish Large Elephant, what we have to do is . . ."

The frog explains her plan to the three companions, and they listen to her very attentively.

The next day, the enormous animal goes for a walk, as he does every day. As soon as she sees him, Striped Bee buzzes, bzz, bzz, bzz, near Large Elephant's ears. He finds this so irritating that he shakes his head wildly in all directions. Taking advantage of his tormented state, Little Bird perches very gently on the big animal's forehead, and then she puts out his eyes with two pecks of her sharp beak.

A terrible trumpeting rings out in the jungle. The blades of green grass in the rice fields bend down over the shimmering water. The flowers close their petals. The birds stop singing. The animals hide. Large Elephant swings his trunk in all directions, beats the ground with his large feet, and is soon surrounded by a thick cloud of dust.

But he does not see that dust because Large Elephant can no longer see anything at all.

Yellow Parrot then flaps his wings and flies around the huge animal, chattering to confuse him even more. At the same moment, the elephant hears, once again, the irritating buzzing of Striped Bee, bzz, bzz, bzz, followed by a croaking, croak, croak, croak.

"Since I can hear the frogs singing," thinks Large Elephant, "there must be water nearby!"

But, in fact, the cunning Green Frog is waiting for him beside a ditch, which a hunter dug the day before. Croak, croak, croak. The enormous animal moves toward her, slips, and falls! Little Bird, Yellow Parrot, Striped Bee, and Green Frog laugh when they see him. His big feet are in the air, his trunk is hanging limply, his tail is tangled up, and his ears are bent back.

"Large Elephant," says Little Bird, "you big, strong, and

handsome master of the jungle, we punished you because you destroyed my eggs. If you promise to go far away from here, and to listen to the cries of the little ones from now on, we will help you out of the ditch."

Desperate to escape from such a bad situation, Large Elephant makes the promise. Then Green Frog guides him out of the trap with his croaking, and leads him back to his herd. Large Elephant rediscovers his companions and, the very next day, he leaves for a distant region in Asia, one that lies far away from Little Bird, Yellow Parrot, Striped Bee, and Green Frog.

Do not despise those who are smaller than you, Large Elephant. Together, they are sometimes much stronger than you might think!

Illustrated by
VIVIANE KOENIG

Apophis the Serpent

With her whole heart, the beautiful Egyptian cow goddess, Hathor, creates the world. She invents night and day, the land, the trees, and flowers, the animals and, shining above all, the great sun god, Ra.

"You will reign forever, my handsome Ra!" she proclaims proudly to her son. Your hot rays will shine on us and I shall protect you. Nobody shall ever be able to do you any harm. Come, my wonderful child, come closer."

Smiling, Ra comes up to his mother with his arms outstretched, and he clasps her in his arms, but she suddenly disappears.

In despair, he weeps so
much that men and women are
born from his tears. Then his mother
appears again. The marvelous goddess
lifts him up between her horns and leads
him down to the vast ocean that
surrounds the Earth. Ra's mouth waters
with happiness and the gods are
born from his lips.

Soon after their birth, all the gods proclaim the glory of Ra and they participate in joyful festivities in his honor. A drop of saliva falls from the mouth of the cow goddess and transforms into a gigantic serpent. This is the birth of Apophis, the brother of the great Ra. His mother takes a quick look at him and then pushes him away, without giving him any further thought. Ra, the son whom she adores, is sufficient to make her happy. He is so hot and so bright!

"Look at that horrible snake! He is crawling over the earth on his belly," mutters one of the gods, in disgust. Apophis shakes his coils sadly. He swings his long tail and blinks. Nobody cares about him. This reptileis unloved, rejected, and despised.

His sorrow turns into a terrible anger, a ferocious jealousy, which will never leave him.

When the great Ra sets foot majestically upon the first island of the world, Apophis pounces and attacks him.

"This ocean and this island belong to me!" he screams furiously.

Then, a terrible fight begins between the two brothers. Armed with a lance, and supported by twenty other snakes, Apophis attacks Ra, who tries to defend himself as best he can by hiding behind a wall of poles. Apophis then strikes the ground violently with his tail and he hurls himself at Ra, ready to devour him. But just then, a god armed with a bow and arrow, a woman with beautiful black hair, and a magician with a shaved head come to Ra's rescue.

"I shall destroy your world, great Ra," mutters the gigantic serpent, as he slithers into the freezing ocean waters. "I shall be avenged. As early as tomorrow, I shall attack you again and this time I shall succeed in destroying you."

Ever since that day, Apophis has been spending his time looking for Ra, the best-loved of the gods. Every morning, he awaits the divine boat that bears the sun god and his faithful companions.

When he sees Ra,
a shiver of envy and hatred
runs the entire length
of his scaled body.

W atch out when I attack, Ra," shouts the serpent, shaking his giant coils. "I will sink your magnificent golden boat that sails across the skies, lights up the world, and warms all humans."

Fortunately, the fish with shining scales is there to alert Ra of the danger. "Watch out!" he cries, as he sticks his big round mouth up out of the water.

"Your wretched serpent brother is on the attack again!"

The crew immediately take up their battle stations. The struggle is fierce, and the golden boat reels about dangerously. Huge waves surround the fighters. This time, one of Ra's companions gains the advantage and wounds the serpent with a final blow of his lance to the serpent's mouth.

"I shall attack you again! I shall sink you," shouts Apophis, as he slips beneath the water. "Soon nobody shall speak of Ra, the sun god, or of his amazing power. I shall win. It may be this evening, tomorrow, or the day after tomorrow, but I shall win."

Never defeated, but never the victor, Apophis relentlessly attacks his hated brother every day.

Neither he, nor the great Ra, will ever win this eternal struggle.

Romulus and Remus

Illustrated by
VÉRONIQUE AGEORGES

When his father dies, the awesome Amulius swears to himself, "I shall be king, instead of my older brother, Numitor, and I shall banish his daughter, Sylvia, forever from my sight. From now on, she will remain in the temple of the goddess of fire. She will never get married and will never have children! This way, no one will ever be able to challenge my place on the throne."

Amulius threatens to kill his brother, and Numitor, who is too scared to defend himself, gives up his right to the throne. His daughter, Sylvia, is led off to the temple of the fire goddess. Now satisfied, Amulius reigns, hunts, and makes war in his kingdom of Tuscany.

But, some time later, Mars, the god of war, notices the beautiful Sylvia as she is fetching some water in the sacred wood.

He immediately falls in love with her, seduces her, and secretly marries her.

Sylvia is soon to have a child. When Amulius hears of this, he swears that Sylvia will die and he throws her into prison. Not long after this, she gives birth to two fine boys, Romulus and Remus, who are snatched violently out of her arms by royal soldiers.

"Sylvia's children must die at once!" the king, who is crazed with anger, orders his servant. "Stab them with your sword, let the wild animals devour them and the waters swallow them up!"

Accustomed to fighting terrible enemies, the faithful servant feels very sorry for these two innocent babies and he is unable to kill them. He sets the cradle down on the river and the current gently carries it off to the opposite bank. It soon comes to rest in some reeds in the shade of a fig tree.

Later that day, a thirsty she-wolf comes down from the mountains to the river. Attracted by the babies' crying, she comes up to them, sniffs them, and very gently offers them her teats. Famished as they are, the two babies suckle for a long time. Day after day, the twins wait impatiently in the shade of the fig tree for the mother-wolf to come.

**As it turns out, the she-wolf has been sent by
the god Mars to look after his children.**

Every morning, she washes them with her tongue, feeds
them with her milk, and then leaves them in the care of a
green woodpecker. He lands on the edge of the basket,
flaps his wings to cool them, removes the leaves that have
fallen on them, and entertains them with his raucous
singing. Then he climbs onto a tree trunk and taps the
bark with his pointed beak. The children laugh when they
hear him.

The two children go on like this until the day a shepherd discovers them and takes them home. The years go by. In the village, Romulus and Remus often fight with the bandits who roam the region. Sometimes they find it more entertaining being bandits themselves, and they steal their neighbors' animals. One day, they attack the shepherds of King Amulius. The shepherds put up a strong fight and succeed in taking Remus to the king as their prisoner.

In the village, all that people are talking about is this terrible incident, and that is how Romulus learns the secret of how he was born.

Immediately, he realizes that his brother is in grave danger. He rushes to the palace, kills the king, and frees Remus. Then he hands power back to his grandfather, Numitor, who was banished such a long time ago by the terrible Amulius.

Having become princes, Romulus and Remus do not really have a place of their own in their grandfather's kingdom. On Numitor's advice, they decide to establish a kingdom in another part of the country, a kingdom that will belong only to them. But who will be the king of the realm? Will it be Romulus or Remus?

They decide that the fairest thing to do would be to listen to the will of the gods. He who sees the greatest number of birds of prey in the sky shall be the victor. By counting the birds in this way, the twins are asking the gods' advice. They watch for the divine "signs" in the sky.

The two brothers walk down to the place where the river washed them up onto the shore in their basket. They are happy to see this beautiful river again, as well as the hill that rises on the bank, and the fig tree, which has now grown tall.

Some birds pass by on the right. Remus counts six vultures, and then Romulus sees twelve of them.

"I shall be king!" shouts Remus with great joy. "I saw the birds first!"

"No, I am the one who shall be king," thunders Romulus. "I am the winner because I saw the greatest number.

"I shall found a city that will bear my name. It will be called Rome!"

Although he is disappointed, Remus accepts his brother's victory.

In order to found his city, Romulus respects the rites laid down by the gods. He first purifies himself by jumping over a brushwood fire. He then digs a ditch and throws into it some soil from the kingdom of his birth. Then, with an instrument shaped like a cross, he takes aim at the sun.

"North is here, East is there," he explains to his brother.

Romulus looks for the four points of the compass to help him decide how to lay out the main streets of the city he plans to build. Finally, he grabs hold of the bronze plow that a cow and a white bull are pulling nearby, digs a trench where the walls are to stand, and marks the location of the temple gates.

"Here are some fine ramparts! I can cross with a single jump!" mocks Remus.

And he hops over the ditch that his brother had just dug.

Exasperated by this insult, Romulus draws his sword and kills Remus. "Let he who attempts to cross my walls die!" shouts Romulus.

That all happened more than 2,700 years ago. Very rapidly, courageous people helped Romulus build Rome's walls, temples, houses, and palaces. Rome became the capital of an immense empire, and the Roman armies made all those who opposed them tremble in fear.

But that, is the beginning of another story.

The Romans have never forgotten that a she-wolf rescued and fed Romulus and Remus. To this very day, her statue stands proudly on top of one of the most beautiful hills in the city.

Illustrated by
DANIEL HÉNON

The Son of Heaven

One day, Assasioua, the son of heaven, is sent by his father to Earth. He arrives in the heart of Africa, and his task is to get some delicious palm wine for his father. Assasioua walks across the plains, where he encounters a herd of elephants, admires some gazelles, and has fun counting the stripes of a few zebras and the patches of some giraffes.

He then enters a village filled with little round huts.

He searches out the chief, who is making preparations for a big festival, and asks him for some palm wine. But the chief is too busy decorating his mask and refuses to share his wine.

Without becoming discouraged, Assasioua walks on for a long time. He listens to the birds singing, disturbs a herd of buffalo, enjoys watching some beetles fighting, and enters a second village made up of little round huts. He goes to see the chief of the village, who is chatting to the head sorcerer, and asks him for some palm wine. But the chief is too involved in his discussions and refuses to give him any.

Still not discouraged, Assasioua walks on even farther. He walks past a pond, where some hippopotami are drinking, admires a flock of pink flamingoes, comes across a sleeping lion, and enters a third village of little round huts. He goes to see the chief of the village, who is playing with his youngest son, and asks him for some palm wine. But the chief is too caught up in his game and refuses to give him any.

Now feeling discouraged, Assasioua turns around and starts to walk along the path leading back to heaven.

It is then that he meets a man returning from a hunt. He asks him for some palm wine and the man gives him some, without asking even the slightest question. This man never asks questions.

"Build a canoe without delay," Assasioua advises the man. "Fill up the holes with mud, set it down straight, and light a fire."

A ssasioua sets off again on the path to heaven, happy that he finally got his father's palm wine.

Without asking any questions, the man chooses a large, solid tree. He cuts it down, digs it out, and shapes it into a huge canoe. A few days later, feeling proud of his canoe but not yet knowing why he needs it, he goes off hunting, hoping to get some further advice. He waits for a long time, a very long time.

One evening, while the man is daydreaming and watching the sun set, Assasioua returns.

L isten to me carefully," says the
son of heaven to the man.
"Soon a torrential rain will fall.
When the crescent moon appears,
climb into your canoe with your wife
and a few animals."

Assasioua smiles at the man and turns
away. Astonished and confused, the man
watches Assasioua drift away along the
path to heaven. He still does not ask
any questions.

On a night darker than any other night he can remember, the man finally sees the small, brilliant crescent amid the stars. He wakes up his wife, and gets into the canoe with her. He also puts his rooster and his hen, his pair of goats, his ram and his ewe, a few other animals he finds near his hut, as well as a lot of others he has caught in the last few days, inside the canoe. As soon as the last animal's last foot is inside, the rain begins to fall.

**Shiny and noisy,
large drops fall from the sky
by the thousands.**

The rain falls for such a long time that
water soon covers the fields, the bush, all of
the houses—large and small—and the
distant forest. It drowns all the humans and
all the animals, except for those in the
canoe. The man watches the rain falling,
not knowing when it will stop, but he still
does not ask any questions.

A ssasioua comes down between the drops of rain and slips into the overloaded canoe and tells the man, "Take this sheet of fabric and stretch it over the canoe like a tent. Then pour the water into your canoe. When the moon next rises, the sun will shine so intensely that you will have to protect yourselves from its hot rays."

As he began to turn away, Assasioua said to the man, "Your palm wine was very delicious."

Before the man knew it, Assasioua had disappeared between the drops of rain.

Without asking any questions, the man sets up the little tent, to protect himself, his wife, and the animals from the sun, and he fills his canoe with water to make it heavier. Soon the next moon rises, and then, for more than two months, the sun no longer goes down; it shines as brightly at midnight as at noon.

The water covering the ground slowly evaporates and eventually disappears altogether.

tepping back onto land, the man builds himself a new hut. He moves into it with his wife, and the animals scatter happily all around it. Soon children are born. They plant crops, raise animals, hunt, and build little huts near their fields.

The children who are born of the man and woman, and all the animals that were saved from the waters, grow numerous and spread to the vast reaches of the Earth. To this day, whenever they drink palm wine, they look up at the sky and they smile.

Are they thinking of Assasioua, the son of heaven, or of the man who unselfishly gave a little palm wine to the unknown traveler?

Illustrated by
VÉRONIQUE AGEORGES

Ulysses and the Sirens

After ten years of bitter fighting, the Greeks finally take the city of Troy. Ulysses, the bravest of their leaders, dreams only of returning to Ithaca, his wonderful little island. Life is pleasant there among the olive trees, the delightfully scented flowers, and beneath a sky that is a deeper blue than anywhere else he has ever seen.

But Poseidon, the god of the oceans, has different plans for Ulysses. And so for many long years, Ulysses undertakes the most extraordinary of epic voyages.

He confronts violent storms
and encounters terrible adversaries—
the Cyclops, a one-eyed giant;
and Circe,
the diabolical sorceress.

One ill-fated day, Ulysses and his sailors
must once again leave dry land.
　　"Let's not waste a moment. Return to
your benches, grab hold of your oars, and cast
off the moorings!" cries Ulysses ardently.

The men obey.
Their oars beat the waves.

The ship rapidly glides away from the shore as the wind fills out its sails. Having reached the high seas, the sailors finally take a rest. Ulysses calls out to them, "My friends, I cannot hide anything from you."

"We must brave a terrible danger before we can return to our beloved Ithaca."

S oon we will have to sail past the land of the Sirens. They are monsters, half-women, half-birds, who sing the most beautiful and enchanting songs."

**"Their voices can drag sailors down
to the depths of the sea."**

"Listen to me carefully. When the right moment comes, you must tie me securely to the ship's mast. I want to hear them singing without being tempted to dive into the dangerous, blue waters. If I beg you to untie the knots that bind me, disobey and fasten them even tighter. Now go back to your places!"

Then Ulysses, a man of unlimited cunning, cuts a large chunk of wax with his dagger. He squeezes and kneads it for a long time between his powerful fingers. He then goes from bench to bench and plugs up the ears of his crewmen. Ulysses then makes a sign to his faithful companions, who tie his arms and legs to the mast. The rope is thick. The knots are firm.

With a strong wind at its back, the ship continues on its course. Suddenly, the breeze subsides, and an eerie calm comes over the sea and the sky. Everything is still. The sailors lower the sails, which are now useless, and they take up their oars once again. As the oars rhythmically strike the water, a white foam appears on the clear, blue waves.

**The Sirens notice the ship
entering their realm.**

They float gracefully through the sky, gliding over the ship and singing a melody that is so beautiful and so sweet that Ulysses is at once captivated.

C ome here, come to us! Ulysses, you whom the people so highly praise. Halt your ship and listen to our voices. No ship has ever sailed past us without listening to the soothing songs that come from our lips. Come Ulysses, come!"

Their wonderful voices fill Ulysses's heart with a tremendous happiness and longing. He struggles against the ropes and gives his crewmen the order to undo the knots that bind him. Bewitched, he struggles and attempts desperately to get loose. Fortunately, the knots do not come undone.

He continues to beg his sailors to set him free, but he is crying in vain.

The sailors can hear neither the magical
voices of the Sirens nor Ulysses's
orders. Bent over their benches, they
plunge their oars into the sea. Seeing how
restless their leader is, his two faithful
companions tighten his bindings to keep him
even more securely tied to the mast.

As the ship sails ahead,
the Sirens become furious
that they have failed
to bewitch these men.

Some hours later, when the sailors are sure that they have sailed far enough away from the dangerous land, they remove the wax from their ears and untie Ulysses. On the horizon they see only sea and sky. Ulysses and his companions still have to face the rest of this long journey. It will be several years before they reach Ithaca, their beautiful island. Many adventures await them before their heroic travels will come to an end.

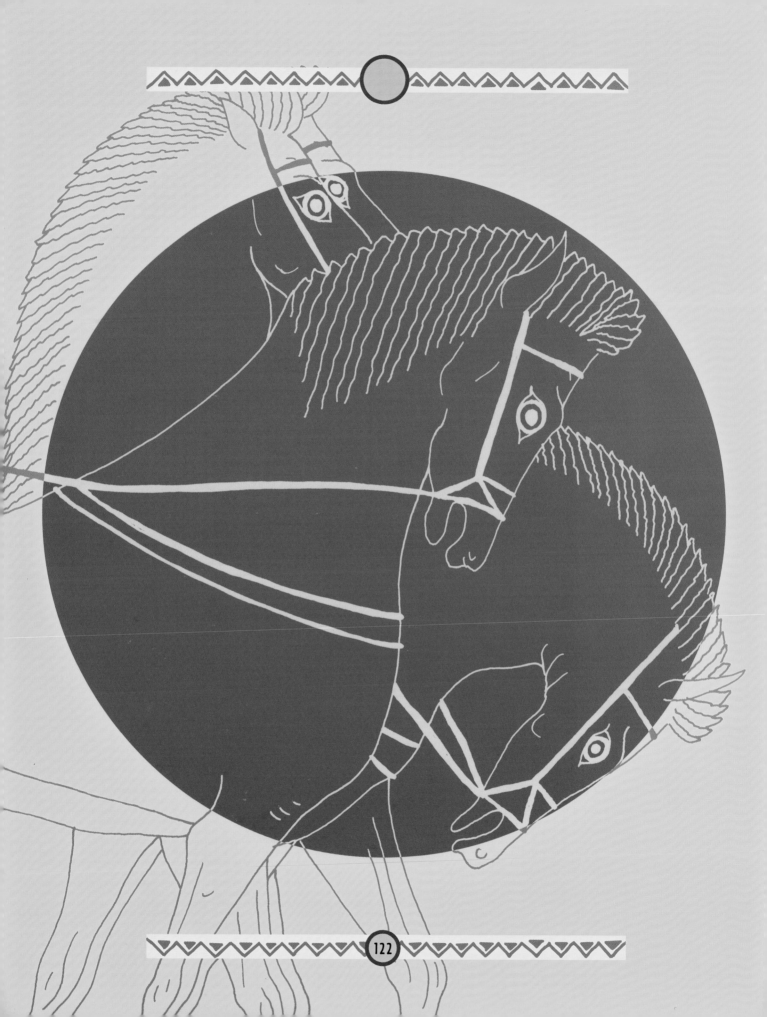

Helios's Chariot

Illustrated by
VIVIANE KOENIG

All Greeks know him well—the brilliant sun god Helios, who rides across the sky in his chariot. "Look, he is passing right over our heads," whisper the women at the well. "Magnificent and proud, he rides in his gleaming chariot of gold, silver, and emeralds!" "He lights up the world, makes the seeds grow,

heats us up in winter, and makes the grapes deliciously golden," proclaim the men, who are sitting in the shade of the olive trees.

Every morning, the brilliant and beautiful Helios leaves his palace of gold and white marble. Its roof is made of ivory, and the doors of silver.

He sets off on his way, which is always strewn with obstacles.

In spite of the monsters and wild animals who attack him, he crosses the sky and pours out his light.

At night, Helios returns to the palace, where he lives with his sisters, Eos and Selene. He rarely sees them because Eos, the dawn who has pink fingers, always travels ahead of him on the heavenly path. As for Selene, the moon, she must leave as soon as he comes home.

When darkness covers the Earth, when the moon and the stars light up the world, Helios is having fun. He dances, laughs, and falls in love so frequently that he forgets the number of women he has loved. Many children have been born as a result of his love affairs.

ut somewhere on Earth, a young man named Phaëthon wonders about the mystery of his birth. For years, people have been making fun of him. "Who is your father? What secret is your mother hiding in her heart?" they constantly ask him.

Some say that he may be the son of the handsome Helios.

Others claim that he is merely the son of an ordinary traveler.

"By the shining rays of this wonderful star, I swear to you, my son, that the sun really is your father," his mother tells him. "If I am lying to you, may this be the last day of my life! If you still do not believe me, go and ask him yourself!"

Phaëthon leaves his house, his city, and his country, and sets off toward the East. He finally arrives at the outer edges of the Earth, where the sun rises. He is thirsty, exhausted, and his heart is pounding. Helios has just come home when the young man enters the great hall, stops some distance away from the god, and bows respectfully. Sitting on his gold and emerald throne, the god listens to Phaëthon's story.

"You really are my son," brilliant Helios assures him with a sparkling smile. "Come closer and do not be afraid."

**"To prove to you that I am your father,
I promise to make whatever you most wish for
come true."**

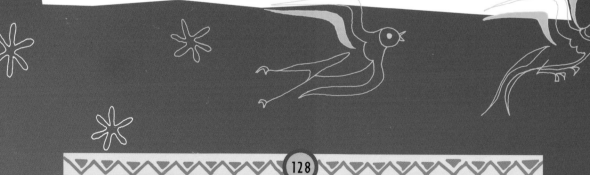

"Oh father! I dream of driving your chariot for one day, just one single day!"

Surprised by such a daring request, the god shakes his luminous head. "My child," he says, "this wish is not appropriate for your age or your strength. The voyage would exhaust you. My horses breathe fire, they rear up and neigh. Many dangers await you on the paths of the sky. You have to pass between the bull's horns and escape the roaring lion and the scorpion's deadly venom. Make a more prudent wish, my son!"

But Phaëthon is not listening and does not understand. He cannot recognize his own youth and his lack of experience.

"I shall be careful and brave," he assures his father, embracing him tightly.

Bound by his promise, Helios leads Phaëthon to the chariot. The dawn approaches as Eos opens the door for him with her delicate, pink fingers.

"It is time. You must follow me," she says to the young man.

Helios pours perfume onto his son's face to protect him from the flames, and he reluctantly holds out the reins.

Standing in the chariot, Phaëthon is not listening to his father's last piece of advice. He crosses the heavy gates of the heavens and ventures happily out onto unknown paths. Phaëthon holds the reins with a firm hand. He crosses silky clouds, sees distant seas and rivers, lands covered with greenery, and cities encircled by white walls. Suddenly, one of the horses bolts. Phaëthon cannot make it obey him.

**The chariot rises
too high,
leaving its proper course,
and tearing the sky.**

Phaëthon panics. His head becomes dizzy and his face gets pale. He no longer dares to look beneath his feet. The Earth, where he lived so happily with his mother, now seems so far away. He regrets his foolish wish.

Suddenly, the monsters his father warned him about rise up in front of him. The roaring lion, the bull with its menacing horns, and the scorpion, dripping its deadly venom and getting ready to sting are all moving nearer. Terrified, Phaëthon lets go of the reins, and the horses rush away, at random, hurling themselves at the stars.

**Alone on the brilliant chariot,
Phaëthon is afraid.**

The horses now begin to plummet toward the Earth. They graze the ground in northern Africa, transforming that region into a barren desert and burning the skin of its inhabitants. Since that day, their skin has remained dark and the desert arid. Overcome by the heat, the earth cracks open, the fields turn yellow, the trees burn, the crops dry up, the seas shrink, the dolphins no longer dare to jump up over the waves.

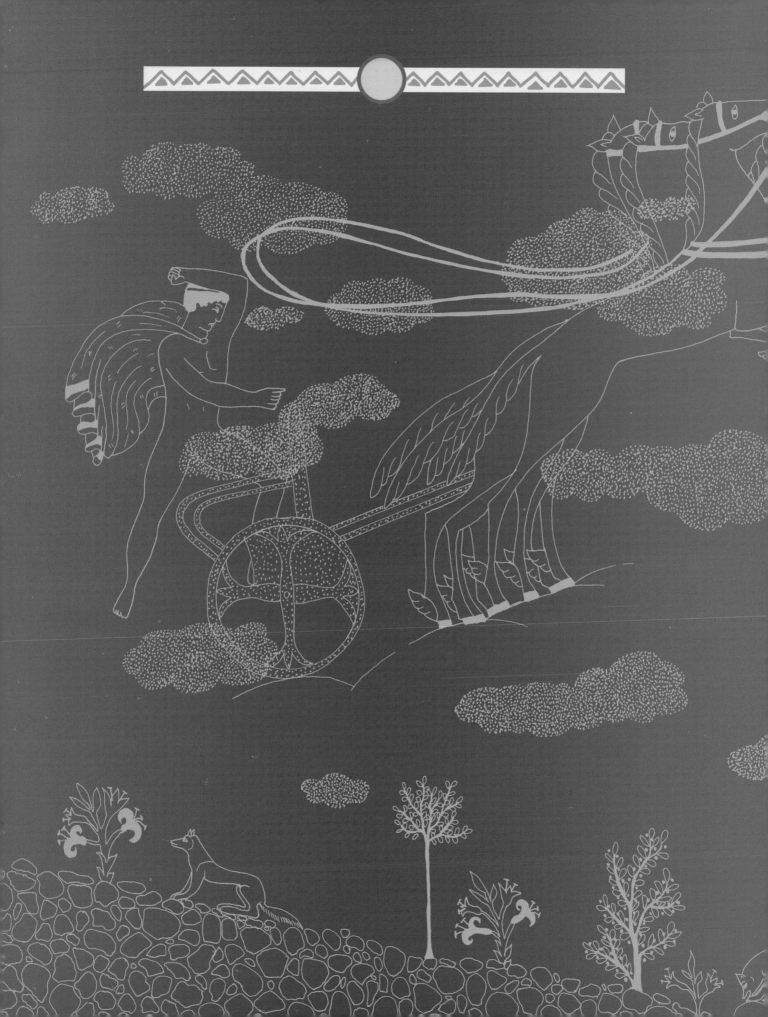

Once again, the chariot rises, climbing higher and higher, and then suddenly falls. Phaëthon then surges forward into terrible and frightening darkness. The Earth trembles and asks Zeus, the king of the gods, to punish the foolish Phaëthon.

"Oh, great god," the Earth laments, "am I going to die because of the stupidity of this ordinary mortal. He cannot take the place of a god. Phaëthon is merely an incompetent fool, and he is burning me horribly."

Without delay, powerful Zeus stands up on the summit of Mount Olympus.

He raises one arm, and sends a thunderbolt to strike down the imprudent youth.

Phaëton's lifeless body then falls, slowly, very slowly, from the sky and crashes to Earth with a dull thud. His sisters rush over to him. They bury him and they weep for their unfortunate brother. They cry so much that they are transformed into poplars, those tall, thin trees that seem to shiver and bend sadly.

In his gold and marble palace, Helios is overcome with grief and hides his face beneath a black veil. One whole day goes by without the sun shining at all. Then he brings together his horses, who are still trembling, reproaches them for causing the death of his son, and then forgives them.

**Ever since this sad adventure,
the sun god has been driving his gold, silver,
and emerald chariot himself,
for it is a chariot that he alone knows
how to drive.**

Tomorrow he will emerge again from his palace in the East. He will cross the entire sky, floating in a gigantic cup of gold on the fluid ocean.

As for the hole Phaëthon tore in the sky, it will never be repaired. It can still be seen on fine summer nights. It is called the Milky Way.

Illustrated by
VIVIANE KOENIG

The Destruction
of Humankind

Thousands of years ago, during the glorious reign of Ra, the young sun god, disorder and evil did not exist on Earth. Everybody had enough to eat, houses did not collapse, thorns did not hurt, snakes did not bite. The gods and humans respected, loved, and obeyed their ruler.

But time passes so quickly. Now that he is old, Ra feels his silver bones cracking and his golden limbs trembling. He sees his lapis-lazuli hair growing pale and he must struggle against feelings of jealousy more and more often. He worries that those envious of his power will attack him. Could they take advantage of his weakness? Do they dream of overturning the world and ruling in his place?

One day, Ra sees a gathering of people in a vast palm grove on the edge of the desert.

Caught up in their discussion, they do not see Ra approaching. He hears them devising a plan to overthrow him and quickly returns to his palace, crazed with anger.

Great gods and mighty goddesses, come and see me without delay. I need your advice," his voice booms.

Everybody rushes to respond to his call. There is old Nun, the sea god, followed by Shu, the air god. Here is Seb, the Earth god, accompanied by Nuit, the goddess of the sky. The ground shakes beneath their feet, causing a storm to rise up on the Very Green Sea. In spite of their giant size, they fall to their knees to bow before Ra. Their brilliant blue hair brushes against the ground.

"Explain to us, oh great god, what is bothering you," they ask at once.

"Men in the palm grove are plotting against me!" Ra explains, with a voice that is shaking with anger.

"I, who created the sky and the Earth for them, who pushed back the greedy waters, who breathed air into their lungs, who invented the plants and animals, the birds and the fish, in order to feed them. Look at those ungrateful wretches! I live among them, I rule over them wisely, and still they want to overthrow me! They deserve a terrible punishment. I fear that they must all be killed."

O h, most powerful of the gods," replies Nun, the sea god, "you will stay on your throne for millions of years. These people who no longer respect you must be punished!"

"Strike them down!"

All the gods voice their agreement with Nun's words. Convinced himself, the master of the world immediately summons Hathor, the goddess with the horns of a bull, and orders her to punish the humans.

H athor transforms herself into a terrible lioness and rushes out of the divine palace. Her fur ruffles up, her teeth sparkle, her tail beats the ground, and her mighty roar echoes throughout the universe. As soon as they see her, the people flee at full speed into the desert. But they can do nothing against Hathor because she always finds them, catches up with them, and kills them.

At the end of the day, proud of the carnage she has caused, Hathor returns to the gods.

"By your life, oh great Ra," says the goddess, "I have acted powerfully and decisively against the humans, and that pleases me immensely. After resting tonight, I shall continue my mission tomorrow."

At that moment, the sun god notices the sparkling eyes of the lioness, the flash of her steel-like claws, her sharp teeth, and her determination. He realizes that if he allows her to continue killing, she will completely destroy humankind. Ra has come to his senses, and he reasons that the punishment seems to have been quite sufficient already.

Without telling Hathor of his plan, Ra decides to save a few humans by using his sense of cunning.

That evening, a great feast is served in the palace. The gods and goddesses enjoy a wide variety of delicious dishes—grilled fish, crisp vegetables, fragrant fruit, exquisite cakes, high-quality beer and wine. They listen to the music of the harpist and admire the female dancers.

After the meal,
the goddess Hathor goes to sleep,
exhausted.

Taking advantage of her sleep, Ra summons his messengers.

"Run to the south of my kingdom," Ra whispers, "and bring me a large quantity of didi, the brilliant red dye that is found only there."

The didi is brought to him, and he orders that it be ground finely. Servant girls mix it with beer and carefully fill seven thousand pitchers with the potion.

"This new brew looks enough like human blood to trick Hathor," declares Ra, with great pleasure.

"Pour this reddish brew all over the ground and we might be able to protect the last humans from that bloodthirsty goddess."

The following morning, the goddess Hathor discovers that the country is bathed in blood. Barely awake but already famished, she crouches down to taste the thick, red fluid. The taste is so pleasing to her that she continues lapping vigorously at the ground. Her head begins to feel light, but she keeps drinking greedily. She ends up drinking so much that she falls into a drunken stupor. Unable to recognize the humans, she staggers home.

Ra is relieved! He has punished the rebels and saved a few humans. But the old god is still disappointed with human-kind and no longer wishes to rule over such ungrateful creatures. It is time for him to leave the Earth and to allow his son, Shou, to take over the throne.

So, Ra summons Nuit, the goddess of the sky, and asks her to lift him up to the heavens, away from the Earth, from its people and its battles. Nuit obeys, raises herself gently, and is soon only touching the Earth with the tips of her fingers and her toes. Before she lifts off completely, her eyes become clouded and her head begins to spin. She is overcome by a terrible dizziness. Ra orders his son to slide under the goddess to support her. Shou obeys and lifts his powerful arms to raise the goddess's belly with the help of eight smaller gods.

Nuit's head clears and she smiles as she watches the gods follow her in the sky one by one.

"We want to live near Ra," they explain. "If he leaves the Earth, we shall leave it too!"

The goddess welcomes them affectionately, counts them, and transforms them into stars.

Ever since that terrible conspiracy took place, and the sun and the other gods left the Earth, people tremble in the darkness of the night.

"Will the sun come back tomorrow to shine on us and to warm us?" they ask every evening, as the golden light disappears below the horizon.

Ra pays little attention to their fears. Every morning he faithfully rises, burning bright and brilliant. And once again, human hearts are happy.

Art direction: Rampazzo and Associates
Editor, English-language edition: Margaret E. Braver
Design Coordinator, English-language edition: Ellen Nygaard Ford

Library of Congress Cataloging-in-Publication Data

Koenig, Viviane.
  [Plus belles histoires de la mythologie.   English]
  A family treasury of myths from around the world / retold by
Viviane Koenig ; translated by Anthony Zielonka ; illustrated
by Véronique Ageorges, Viviane Koenig, Daniel Hénon.
          p.   cm.
    ISBN 0–8109–4380–8 (hardcover)
    1. Mythology.   I. Title.
  BL311.K6413   1998
  398.2—dc21   98–16739

Printed and bound in Belgium

 Harry N. Abrams, Inc.
100 Fifth Avenue
New York, N.Y. 10011
www.abramsbooks.com